RALLY CAR RACING

BY ANITA BANKS

APEX

WWW.APEXEDITIONS.COM

Apex is distributed by North Star Editions:
sales@northstareditions.com | 888-417-0195

Produced for Apex by Red Line Editorial.

Photographs ©: Shutterstock Images, cover (car), 1 (car), 4–5, 6–7, 8, 9, 10–11, 12–13, 14–15, 16–17, 18, 19, 20–21, 22–23, 24–25, 26, 27, 29; Pixabay, cover (background), 1 (background)

Library of Congress Control Number: 2021915733

ISBN
978-1-63738-153-3 (hardcover)
978-1-63738-189-2 (paperback)
978-1-63738-259-2 (ebook pdf)
978-1-63738-225-7 (hosted ebook)

Printed in the United States of America
Mankato, MN
012022

NOTE TO PARENTS AND EDUCATORS

Apex books are designed to build literacy skills in striving readers. Exciting, high-interest content attracts and holds readers' attention. The text is carefully leveled to allow students to achieve success quickly. Additional features, such as bolded glossary words for difficult terms, help build comprehension.

TABLE OF CONTENTS

CHAPTER 1

READY SET

Rally car drivers **rev** their engines. Swirls of dust fill the air. Excited fans wait for the race to begin.

Rally car drivers often start at different times. The second driver might start a couple minutes after the first.

The **official** signals the start. The cars speed down the road. The first car slides around a curve. Then the driver shifts **gears** and goes faster.

ON THE ROAD

Rallies happen on public roads. But roads are closed during the race. The roads can be paved, dirt, or gravel. They may also have mud, sand, or snow.

During a race, rally cars can go 100 miles per hour (161 km/h).

A **co-driver** sits in the passenger seat. He tells the driver what lies ahead. They race toward the **checkpoint**.

A co-driver reads notes about the race to the driver.

Many rallies in Northern Europe have lots of snow.

Rally car racing takes place year-round. The weather may be hot, cold, rainy, or snowy.

CHAPTER 2

AT THE START

The first rally car races started in the early 1900s. The Monte-Carlo Rally began in 1911. Drivers began in different parts of Europe. The finish line was in Monte Carlo, Monaco.

Rallies still take place in Monte Carlo, Monaco. Monaco is a small country on the coast of France.

Rallies became more popular after World War II (1939–1945). Drivers from around the world started racing one another. They used sections of roads as their courses.

The Hotchkiss was the winning car of the 1949 Monte-Carlo Rally. The race was the first in years because of World War II.

36
RVE MONTE-CARLO

686-RS-37

In early races, cars often went less than 9 miles per hour (14 km/h).

The World Rally Championship began in the 1970s. The world's best racers compete in it. Today, rallies take place in many countries.

The World Rally Championship holds 13 races each year. They are in more than 10 countries.

THE OLYMPUS RALLY

The Olympus Rally is held near Seattle, Washington. The racecourse has many twisting turns. It winds through the forest.

CHAPTER 3

STAGE RALLIES

Most rallies have stages. Each stage is a section of road. Drivers who go through it the fastest score points.

Each stage of a rally is often 50 to 250 miles (80–402 km) long.

Many stages have **hazards**. Drivers often learn about them the day of the race. Co-drivers get notes. They tell the drivers what to look for.

Dangerous surfaces are common hazards in rallies.

Snow can be a hazard in winter rallies. Drivers can get stuck.

Rallies can have more than 20 stages.

Drivers travel to the next stage. Then they race again. The car with the most points at the end wins.

A driver turns through a desert in Saudi Arabia during the 2020 Dakar Rally.

The longest rally was 18,000 miles (29,000 km) long. It took almost three months.

DESERT DRIVING

The Dakar Rally is held in Saudi Arabia. It is a desert race. Drivers cover thousands of miles of rough ground. Cars often crash or break down.

CHAPTER 4

RALLY CARS

Rally cars are built for tough road conditions. People **enhance** the cars' engines. That gives the cars more power.

A regular car can be changed into a rally car.

Rally cars use wide tires. The tires also have thick **tread**. This helps cars grip the road.

An important member of any rally team is the mechanic. He keeps the car ready. Sometimes he is also the driver.

A rally car's tires help it make sharp turns on rough roads.

Roll cages protect the drivers and co-drivers. Good **suspension** is also important. It absorbs bumps to make the ride smoother.

A roll cage goes around the area where the driver and co-driver sit.

Good suspension helps
rally cars keep racing
after big jumps.

CAR TALK

There is a lot of noise during a rally race. So, the

driver and co-driver use an **intercom**. That way,

they don't have to shout to hear each other.

COMPREHENSION QUESTIONS

Write your answers on a separate piece of paper.

1. Write a sentence that explains the main idea of Chapter 3.

2. Would you like to drive in a rally car race? Why or why not?

3. What part of a rally car helps it grip the road?

    A. its wide tires

    B. its suspension

    C. its roll cage

4. Why would a mechanic be an important part of a rally team?

    A. The driver needs help steering the car.

    B. The rough course means the car is likely to crash or break down.

    C. The many stages make it easy for cars to get lost.

5. What does **compete** mean in this book?

*The World Rally Championship began in the 1970s. The world's best racers **compete** in it.*

    A. to lose an event

    B. to stay away from an event

    C. to try to win an event

6. What does **absorbs** mean in this book?

*Good suspension is also important. It **absorbs** bumps to make the ride smoother.*

    A. lessens something

    B. makes something bigger

    C. makes something louder

Answer key on page 32.

GLOSSARY

checkpoint
The end of a stage in a race.

co-driver
A passenger who helps with driving.

enhance
To make stronger or greater.

gears
Settings on cars that control how fast cars can go.

hazards
Things that can put people in danger.

intercom
A device involving speakers and microphones, which allows two people to talk to each other.

official
A person who works for a group or event.

rev
To make an engine speed up and work harder.

suspension
The tires, springs, and other parts of a car that connect the car to the wheels.

tread
The part of a tire that touches the road.

TO LEARN MORE

BOOKS

Hale, K. A. *Rally Car Racing*. Minnetonka, MN: Kaleidoscope, 2019.

Roselius, J Chris. *Superfast Rally Car Racing*. Minneapolis: Lerner Publications, 2020.

Shaffer, Lindsay. *4x4 Trucks*. Minneapolis: Bellwether Media, 2019.

ONLINE RESOURCES

Visit **www.apexeditions.com** to find links and resources related to this title.

ABOUT THE AUTHOR

Anita Banks lives in North Alabama. She loves reading and running. She also loves to travel and learn new things.

INDEX

Answer Key:
1. Answers will vary; **2.** Answers will vary; **3.** A; **4.** B; **5.** C; **6.** A